CASCADES

JOAN CANBY

ASSURE PRESS

Copyright © 2021 by Joan Canby

All Rights Reserved. No part of this book may be performed, recorded, used or reproduced in any manner whatsoever without the written consent of the author and the permission of the publisher except in the case of brief quotations embodied in critical articles and review.

An imprint of Assure Press Publishing & Consulting, LLC

www.assurepress.org

ASSURE PRESS

Publisher's Note: Assure Press books may be purchased for educational, business, or sales promotional use. For information please visit the website.

Cascades/ Joan Canby— 1st ed.

ISBN-13: 978-1-954573-06-2
Library of Congress Control Number: 9781954573062
eISBN-13: 978-1-954573-07-9

THANKFUL ACKNOWLEDGEMENTS

Stan Zumbiel

Lisa Chang and the Hybrid Poets

CONTENTS

Cascade #1 At the Altar	1
Cascade #2 The Astronomer's Questions	2
Cascade #3 The Quarrel	3
Cascade # 4 Search	4
Cascade #5 Suburbia	5
Cascade # 6 Stockholm's Djuargarden	6
Cascade # 7 Prayers to Pagan gods	7
Cascade #8 Love Remembered	8
Cascade # 9 Curiosity	9
Cascade #10 Writing	10
Cascade #11 Scaled Knives	11
Cascade #12 Sugar	12
Cascade #13 Rogue Wave	13
Cascade # 14 Adrift	14
Cascade # 15 Pelican	15
Cascade #16 Plein Air Painter	16
Cascade # 17 Train Ride	17
Cascade # 18 Watercolors at the Beach	18
Cascade #19 Birdbath	19
Cascade #20 Outliers	20
Cascade #21 Recovery	21
Cascade #22 Straw	22
Cascade # 23 Leftover	23
Cascade #24 Unchanged	24
Cascade #25 Mourning	25
Cascade # 26 Dancing	26
Cascade # 27 Twins	27
Cascade #28 Drop Off	28
Cascade # 29 Jansen's Art History	29
Cascade # 30 Solar Eclipse of the Sun	30
Cascade #31 Atoll	31
Cascade # 32 Astronomer alone	32
Cascade #33 Jibe Ho	33
Cascade #34 Cranes	34
Cascade #35 Day of the Memorial	35
Cascade #36 Flight	36
Cascade #37 Pasture	37
Cascade #38 Day Person	38
Cascade #39 Chopin's Prelude B Minor	39

Cascade #40 Sentimental	40
Cascade #41 Competition	41
Cascade #42 Gambler	42
Cascade #43 Gallery Opening	43
Cascade #44 Kite Flying	44
Cascade #45 The Visit	45
Cascade #46 Flamenco	46
Cascade #47 Know Your Knots	48
About the Author	49

CASCADES

Cascade #1 At the Altar

Stained glass light, a full moon reflecting on a pond full of prayers,
        light dancing in double-quick time, performing
staccato cartwheels as friends entered, bowed, kneeled, glanced left

to right. She wanted to hear a sea lion's bark, a train whistle's hunger,
        to know another searched for her like a new moon
waiting for a sunrise. After they walked down the aisle they pulled

chapel bells, held the woven rope coil their hand's together,
        bells peeling within a nocturne light
of sprinkled mist. She in white peau de soie, Chantilly lace,

holding a gardenia bouquet, he with a sailor's stopwatch tucked
        into white damask. Later the honeymoon at sea,
later a carnation lei thrown into the waves. Later she fell into

dead air trying to reach for buttered bread when her life
        crushed as under ten feet of snow
to collapsing, then, her cry drowned by wind and wave.

Cascade #2 The Astronomer's Questions

A skylark preens on a sloop's sail rigging,
        not penned in,
ready to lift off into the horizon,

while her lost husband on his tropical isle scans the night's sky,
        Europa moons, for Titan and Enceladus.
He asks are there new Eves, new Adams, another Noah creating their arks?

Will they embrace our books, cherish our Michelangelo?
        Will life survive through the grace of starlight suns?

He's a collector of stars, their light his sliding door to council,

to friendship to understanding. A surf board stands next to his bed,
        an espresso machine brews.
Glasses on his nose, his hand on the telescope tube looking as free as a skylark.

She asks what about the void, the darkness of the sky, if it's enough.

Cascade # 3 The Quarrel

When strength wraps tight as a panther's
        muscle before it pounces,
a first love's kiss lurches into a new life,

boulders roll away and they lift up to the sky,
        letting the honeybees loose
to find their hive, allowing silence's secret hum –

gifts given, when woven back into their wool's
        warmth, then a dewdrop fades
into the sun. Dull blades pierce wood, a magnolia's

rubber white blossom opens like returning into memory,
        like a proud crane standing on one leg
waiting for fish. A grey-eyed wolf still listens, smells air's

danger like wife and husband surviving their differences,
        avoiding their contempt.

Cascade #4 Search

Escaping great old peculiars like love and lemon blossoms
        marinating in Valencia orchards, she is
resolved to go to China far from fallen lemons, into another

world of walls, another language and other stones. If she
        stirs up her days, to catch dragonflies,
if she allows sweet peas to bloom tangled in cotton strings

and gardenia waxy bloom, accepts detached holes with
        their flowering hope. As if China takes her
ponderous body in, tells her their secrets then she'll sit

at their table, no longer the imposter, no longer
        not as good as, she'll call off her search.

Cascade #5 Suburbia

Blue sky mirrors a swimming pool in backyard suburbia where
        a heron perches stalwart as a treble clef on a scale
preening his magical surprise changing into light, in her dream a

monster gargoyle perches at the foot of her bed shunning her lyrical
        page while outside cumulus hover above herons,
pool and bed. Then, their children balance on the diving board then leap

to make triple-back flips touching the circle of oak tree limbs then
        to return to water. Elsewhere, the Eucalyptus speak
and the Sycamores reply -- a serenade begins as green parrots agree

she will find their landing, even if, flight is for the heron not for them.

Cascade #6 Stockholm's Djuargarden

Like a sailboat in irons she left with the stranger moved like
        a jib away from empty rooms, telescopes and
painter's easels, a bow away from grief's wind elsewhere to

Sweden's islands to walk in Djurgarden with its Baltic Sea
        views, where deer hid, where Jenny Lind's statue
and soprano memory sang amongst flowered beds of forget-me-nots.

She wore a blue silk dress as she leaned back on the narrow
        toughened trunk of a birch tree touching its
twisting, swirling grey-white bark to see a mystical white-feathered

swan floating in the archipelago. It struggled to escape
        from gravity. It lifted, dragged its web feet
tightened, toughened black claws touching together,

the indivisible wind above the wings fighting gravity. Pushing
        forward faster lifting, cancelling gravity, it rose
up -- the swan took off. It powered forward, beat its wings,

flapping, flapping then flapping into a wide embrace of air
        teaching her in blue to watch for, then to witness grace.

Cascade #7 Prayers to Pagan gods

It is Ibis who judges. Away from the puzzles, the broken pieces,
        a jackal smells for the dead while the cassia,
juniper berries, camphor oil and incense smoke fills the air as the

jackal speaks to them. A simple answer to mystery the cloud breaks away
        from sleep then crosses over bridges into the disarray
world. Bruises brown as character stiffens, bricks up, loosens like after new
rain,

releasing an unwelcomed withered peel, forgiveness as far away
        as a Tahitian moon where pekaki leis brown and the
drones harsh wind's blow and sarcasm bites the hook, then a jackal proceeds

to weigh hearts. If feather light, life promised, if too heavy damnation. Her
pleas   rise to Saraswati the goddess of everything that flows, water,
words,
melody praying the streams of cascading kindnesses grace first her boys,
then his

stars, then dew on the leaves below. He listens for stars whisper while his wife
        prays for their lost children in the darkness of their bed.
Her mission to be a mother, his drive to find a new star, both knew themselves

but not the fickle other. Awake without a Russian sable brush in hand, she
        looked for the reflected light in the shadows then scanned
his sleeping face a mirror to her own then prays for mercy's judgment.

Cascade #8 Love Remembered

She remembered loving him like a brown-spotted
        hen enjoying her dust bath and
white doves flying free into the hushed air and cloud.

She marveled remembering his smile like sitting within
        an oak's tree world a canopy of thick
clotted leaves, squirrels, lichens, ferns, fungi sharing latticed

sun-light with robins, woodpeckers, and redstarts
        no complaints among the species,
branches embracing outward open and generous to all

like their first embrace. Fire melts glass down into a brass
        vessel holding, not breaking apart transforming
to create, to shimmer a new crystal life like a new wife making

chicken soup and matzo taking a deep breath, patting the baby,
        leaving old anger to burst open releasing her,
holding infant, folding flour balls. When the low light of morning

scuttles the clouds, when the sun-bright snow, barn hides in blue-gray
        shadow, when windows shut a cold crisp air aglow, he in
reflected light babbles, she in her mourning they hold their hands together.

Cascade #9 Curiosity

She asks if plants sing as they bloom and stones wail when lovers die.
        Asks if her husband saw starlight when he held his child
cold and blue. Asks if she sees holy light when she sees the sea, when

the memorials pass away. When the eulogies fade into the silent air,
        when sister, brother, friend depart, then alone, to avoid,
to distract with book, film, wine, she chooses not to question. She stops

asking, if whether it will rain tomorrow, if whether the postman will come today,
        if whether the plumeria needs to come in from the storm.
She stops asking the how. She stops inquiring the when. Never more will she ask
        the why, like Lot's wife, she accepts the salted pillar.

Cascade #10 Writing

She can cook, see words, paint sounds,
        while elsewhere deer, antelope,
gazelle roam, her pale yellow page once white
        changes in blue ink like braised
buttered meat, her life in a medium oven shimmering.

Azure, celeste, lapis lazuli sky a veil in mourning
        her gaze moved up to a broad blue
sky as she prepares the order for their memorial plaques
        to pay for them with her Mother's inheritance.

She paid for her coming in she can pay for her boys
        going out. Her Mother pickled her
brain at her age while here she writes in blue arpeggios.

Cascade #11 Scaled Knives

Pencil smears scaled lines, a binder of notes, details tangle
        tied together, if she loosens the pages, then allows
them to fly to the ground, if her grandfather had dropped the
        serrated knife when her grandmother ran out on Mesa Drive,

let the metal tone of the knife sing as it fell hitting the road not her,
        as if the marriage was not over. How many more years
was her own throat throttled? When she was held by her husband's
        tapered Marine's thumb at the small of her throat?

She did not run. No binder or child left behind to tell. She allowed
        cinnamon specks to sink into her coffee cream, offered breakfast
coffee to him. Today she sorts binders, utensils and spice memories, then
        looks out to see her solitary garden where tulips begin to unfold

like a peacock's tail, watches herself in her silver-backed mirror with its jagged
        edge its broken handle, then separates from them as she sits,
plays, listens to chord progressions, jazz riffs, left-over scales between
        grandmother, grandfather, husband, lost boys.

Cascade #12 Sugar

Sensual sugar, sweet endings of chocolate,
        grounding them alongside
espresso and milk to relax forgetting the back
        hand, the white man's whip,
the cane plantation fields of cruelty. Sweet
        sugar celebrates, consoles, melts
into mouths, the ultimate sweet state of their
        storied stories, their sweet grief.

Cascade #13 Rogue Wave

A fishing boat keels towards the horizon and like
        a sighing third in Brahms last
symphony, a cello's masculine song vibrates between
        the Channel Islands where her two boys
drowned, taken by a rogue wave – now hidden, abducted
        by a horizon where the light ends.
She stretches her arm up, as if, a thin musical line separates
        her from the sea graves, as if, to signal,
        here I am. Come back. Come back to me.

Cascade #14 Adrift

The stranger's fist inside his black wool pocket tightens
        as they walk on the beach beside stone,
tree, water. They wait for the silent wind to speak, to tell

them to leave pleasing places to arrive at knowing places.
        Back home to drink cognac continuing on to
ragu and gumbo, old talk diminishes to a faded hazy grey,

car headlights blare into their windows from the approved road.
        When the sparring, spewing angry venom belches
to collide into silver cascades like within the wave and rubble

tossing, reeds, glass, when the downward swoop of a pelican catches
        the halibut, sea's holy gift, feeds, then the wing
swells the wave, then they're left adrift, then they're left alone.

Cascade #15 Pelican

Descending a staircase not falling, not tripping
          down, as love trickles like water
in a fountain, waterfalls into a pond and their love

once as big as the weather, once as joyful as a
          butterfly's flutter, once as real as
amethyst skies at noon, dwindles, diminishes,

vanishes. No anger remains. No betrayals' lies
          linger. Continents separate them then a
morning arrives when a pelican swoops down

into the sea for its prey to carry it away, to feed
          alone. She wanted it to gather her up
into its beak, to transport her too, to change her.

Cascade #16 Plein Air Painter

When she leaned forward right-arm extending
        firm thrust out like a conductor
with her flat brush to smooth, to blend the feathered

leaves her right foot placed in the same position
        she stood in flamenco class, then she
begins to breath in the grey trunk of the Bur Oak,

glides her eye to view six shades of green, speckled
        water droplets on firm grey branches,
when she refuses to hear the chatter of the eighty year

salesman, the retired kindergarten teacher, propping up
        their easels as they take their quills, shaders,
fan blenders, squirrel fans to recreate the oak, make it alive,

when she forgets her story, when everything has changed,
        her tree straight ahead like the day she walked out
from him, closed the garage door, drove to the sacred grove.

Cascade #17 Train Ride

A running pencil gallops through her lap-held
        journal, a rasping line of outlines,
images to protect her like a roof shingle or an

umbrella quarreling with the hail, her pencil in hand
        she sketches as her train slides through
on its track by the Pacific Ocean beside the San Gabriel

Mountain Range, she's living in haze time like the seagull
        perched on a cliff waiting for sunset's ruby-crusted
horizon-line. A lead pencil looks for wisdom shadings, lines

to create not to dissolve into separation and disruption.
        From her fogged smeared window her train
passes a party of twelve sitting on garden furniture with their

champagne flutes held by women wearing pink. Her train passes
        the vision of window glamour gaiety as she cuddles,
coaxes her pencil to praise her, to admire her, to feel less than.

Cascade #18 Watercolors at the Beach

Water combines paint finding form,
        design, accepting water's mistakes
letting paint and water marry as walkers,

swimmers, couples stroll looking down their worn,
        crimped, anxious faces snatching up
a scallop shell, a piece of green sea glass, an abandoned

black clam, between kelp nodules. Does the half-shell
        clam wonder how it lost its twin?
The watercolor painter leans her head against a rock

headboard cradling her hair, the silky air soothing
        her watered down spirit listening to
the ocean singing to her with each wave falling one

crest upon another. When she lifts her brush remembering
        immediate will flee when the merging
blues and greens slide together not catch the sea, beach, rock

on the page, when failing to create she lets the
        water immerse, soak, kidnap
then cleanse, the page, the brush and then her.

Cascade #19 Birdbath

Water fountain basin for sparrows, chickadees
        and blue jays, a vision for prayer,
a place for pondering with Earl Grey tea in-hand

until a reckless lover buried her fountain in earth,
        and succulents. No need for water,
like the songbirds, like her, like Noah. After Noah

drove the pitch into an ark of gopher wood to save
        songbirds, to save breathe, after Noah
let loose the raven, after the dove returned with an olive

branch, after Noah created wine as if water, when birdsongs
        answered, when water dampened her pleasures,
when jade, desert rose and aloe vera rooted in her basin,

her beloved tasks no longer mattered. Then like Noah's present
        of a rainbow, she believed, her laundry, washing
yellowed jerseys, throwing the idle toy trucks aside, to create

new lines her waiting for her promise, for her rainbow.

Cascade #20 Outliers

Raccoon tail, black and white striped tail, a diamond back rattlesnake
    hidden in a black hole in the red dirt canyon wall
rattle sparring, tongue hissing, a rattle snake round-up with ten men

circling five snake dens, white garden sprayer full of gasoline,
    attached to an aluminum coil tube, flashlights in hand,
fuming, gassing the dens harvest yellow-pus venom to save bitten man.

Captured gassed, rounded up, weighed, killed, skinned, venom bottled
    outliers are taken. The serpent snakes caused
the ouster. Snakes thrown out like the limestone, sandstone, quartz,

each piece not perfect for the secular museum church the imperfect not
    used for the wall, set aside, apart like the snake, as
when you said, "I'm lecturing. You don't have children any more you

don't know," silent, bowed with her empty womb, she's skinned like a snake.

Cascade #21 Recovery

When a silver moon like a loose slipper rose
        after the sun set, after his afternoon
of kneeling, paddling his surfboard parallel to the

coastline looking for the next wave, he never turned back,
        to look at her, to look at the moon. When
she left her house where sadness shadows smelled beside

creased curtains where pet stains remained on yellow carpet,
        and brown metallic TV trays by her chair
and plastic pill bottle cemeteries, when she bent her neck, her chin

leaned forward, as if she knew secrets while she spoke of sage,
        of rituals of incense, and evil daemon nets where
light fell through then outside the winds gathered the sea into

waves of applause, no longer a victim, a gun in her purse, not
        an adverb, no longer a noun she arranged her tear
gas canister and gun in her purse her speech numb like a beached

dolphin with too much oxygen and her heart bandage
        lifted from its wound, blood healed to
reveal she is alive like a blade of grass without GMO.

Cascade #22 Straw

On smooth rush chairs on top of a jute twisted rope rug
        their plates on silky sea grass mats, they eat
while their lives shake like straw, fragmented and loose.

No sailor's abaca rope, braided into a chunk woven strong
        to tie their rigging to continue their sailing.
As she picks at her chicken she wonders about leaving his

prepositions, *his next to, beside, beholden to, alongside*,
        for a new conjunction world to join *also,*
nevertheless, and new *ands*. While his life erodes like a

threatened cliff when earth, grass, worm plunge, skid into
        a tumble, free-falling into the sea's arms, were there
cascading waterfalls in Genesis beside the knowledge tree?

He reaches for her hand across the table, plate, a childless couple
        left aside to linger at the door, where roles
and hopes kick up to the sky, solitary like pieces of straw with

no child to tell who they are. Who they might have been.

Cascade #23 Leftover

Earth in its dark amber, in its perverse musk,
        where triumphant hyacinth's evening
scent rises as earth revolves around the sun,

while her husband left behind scans the sky
        to search the same expanse as the Pole
Copernicus, the Dane Brahe, the Italian Galileo

as their love expanse mellows like an oboe receding
        into memory. Once he understood the
routine of waking, morning coffee, showers together,

their night's leftovers, books closed, photographs abandoned.
        Once he filled vases full to cascading dozens of
yellow roses. Once he wanted the yellow petals to plead for

forgiveness, for her to return, for them to try again. Then he
        forgot her scent, her voice's lilt at the table,
her step opening into the foyer, returned to his telescope's

tube letting the vision of her in periwinkle blue recede
        as he became a leftover under house arrest.
While she watches water drip into the earthen basin, smoothes

it with palm and finger the red-brown soil like their boy
        after his bath when his toe met towel,
she takes the tea rose leftover root ball pushes it downward.

Cascade #24 Unchanged

Scar pecked alive, like the sparrows
        pecking through a pine
wooden sill looking for seed to live,

while her heart searched for a fragrance
        in an unblemished gardenia,
an angel-dusted orchid, waiting for

the red Bordeaux wine to rest like a friendship
        taken, drunk from, then spent.
Until Sunday morning arrives, when she will

boil the egg, when he will compute the numbers
        to the skies and outside the wild
yellow mustard dances, kisses the air in the same

way as the day before, the red-tailed hawk will fly
        into the sycamore in the same way as a
month before, the sea will sparkle in the same way

as the day in January the year before but they are not
        as they once were before, before, then.

Cascade #25 Mourning

He searches to the skies. She searches the arch of a branch,
        the sweep of a petal through her brush.
Their answer – grace ends in water. A life like an oak's

roots tell of miles below unknown until uprooted and gone.
        Her dish towel rung to let the water out,
her grief drains, no time for drying, rung like a chicken's head,

then limp, then plucked feathers, then bare skin opened for the caress
        of salt, the pepper mill black speckled pocked death scab.
Her plea to Harbor master, *Where are they? Why haven't they come back?*

Then the police at the door, then the red tractor, Thomas the train,
        Lego men tumbled into red, green, yellow heaps
inside the empty fireplace, idle like her husband's telescope blinded

by dust, outside the sea, no roots to unearth, ashes to spread, no flowers to cover.

Cascade #26 Dancing

Her father's long tapered fingers gave her dance
    cues to go right, to go backward
fingers at the small of her back, glided her into a waltz,

his cheek-grizzled and rough against hers. The first man
    she loved, the first man who loved her,
in her first cascade waltz directed into circles on parquet lace.

Then her husband's shifty, sexy moves, shimmy in time sway,
    then the melody changed again, replaced
by ocean air current drifting, wafting in fog waves of grey

then they stopped dancing, ceased searching, stripped
    silent, stilled as their windmill sailboat.

Cascade #27 Twins

Across the horsehairs the bow draws vibrates, tightens strands
        the violinist loosens the bow as she listens,
she takes her paint tube of crushed oregano green, watches it

spool from the tube and sit on her palette against the violet
        shadow as a radio violinist plays. She chose
to unwrap the cool white with its blue hoping for brightness.

She looks out criss-crossing meadows towards the sea with its
        palette of Indian paintbrush, mustard and spring
laughing lupine wishing for lust, wrath and hubris, preferring

passions than the cold grief of the empty bunk beds inside. Water
        laps at their dock, brown planks breathe while waves
watch twilight before the stars open to the sky to close their sentences

to silence not talking their trouble their terror breaking them in two.
        They who celebrated their twin lives, their twin toes,
locked under sage green linen sheets after creating two tow headed

curly bobs, their twins. Their boys, locked within water, not healing,
        water never knowing their names to forget. Weeks pass.
A white-tailed deer, fleet fast, its tip-toe hoofs cross their Mexican red-dust

tile into the dead bedroom with its double bunk beds, empty, unchanged,
        resting for a return until they never return, until the white
tailed deer appears, peers inside. She awakes, hears the tinkle of frightened

hooves. Screams. Plantation fans switches on to lighten, white paddles swirl
        attacks the air, to detach the heat, deer to flee.

Cascade #28 Drop off

Inside her father's front door she stood on a Persian garden carpet
        woven silk threads of figures, one youth near
flowering acacias trees, a resting gazelle, a flying pheasant in white.

She bent, leaned down to the one's sneakers, and then pat another's foot,
        she gazed down at the figures in the rug of gazelle, tree,
pheasant then her boy. She stood up as her father picked up one kissed

his cheek and then with his wide flat palm crossed the face of the older
        one as if a puppy. As if they were his beloved black
Stallion corralled behind their house, his house, her childhood place.

She left them to go together to attach jib to headstay, cleat
        and coil, lines to jib sheets to clew and
lead to winch. She waved them good bye to sail into the wind.

Cascade #29 Jansen's Art History

On their balcony as speaker phone rumbles to tell the tale, he talks,
        comforts, neighbor, colleague hawk in the distant
afternoon sky hears nothing, continues to fly, she inside scans Jansen's

Art History looking at Madonnas. Where were their life jackets? No bodies found.
        Once like Fra Filippo Lippi's Madonna she held a babe in her lap
and his chubby hand touched her at her neck caressed her as she held him by the waist.

Were the three vests found floating the only remains of children and father?
        She turns the page to Winslow Homer's Gulf Stream,
sharks on the stern, a ship on the horizon, sea gusts, storm in the distance

no ship arrives to save, better resolve herself. Turns the page to Cezanne's basket
        of apples undisturbed, unblemished, unspoiled, uneaten.
Gasping for air, their lungs full as the night sky opening to the constellation of Capricorn,

Venus appearing in Sagittarius and Jupiter the happy abundant planet shining
in   Aires as Neptune overtaken by the water Aquarian sign like them.

Cascade #30 Solar Eclipse of the Sun

Glass protectors shielded the eyes of her boys, their grandfather
        as they waited on plaid wool blankets looking
up for the sun's celestial pas de deux, as midday light faded

then the moon slunk in front of the sun, a shadow appearing,
        an umbra, the sky's umbrella embrace,
to engulf Sivas, then shadow nears as the moon fronts the sun,

a ghostly pearl white halo ascends the moon's perimeter.
        Eyes upward as the moon slides as if the sky's
deep dark blue horizon sighed messages, as if in angel light,

as if a dance to the halo, a seven-year eclipse, for their seven
        year-old boys. Did the jib hit them? Did they
lean over as the wind waltzed the boat through wave upon wave,

like a pebble skimming water from north to horizon?
        Did the sigh of the sea breathe them in
as they slipped overboard? Who saw the wave that cast

towed-haired boys into the sea? Did a seagull? Did the sun?

Cascade #31 Atoll

A Caesarean scar divides flesh across her body like how the land
        ends and the ocean begins, how a wave moves in
and out, how the pull of the moon shifts water's level, how the shore's

earth erodes by waves and tides to combine, change hour by hour,
        six hours, then six days, finally, six months pass.
Abandoned parents alive on a half-shore, half-ocean zone, half-mourning,

half-grief releasing attempting to live like mangrove trees in seawater
        to expand from seafloor trapping sediments to create
new land to create a new life with new stars to see, new trees to paint.

She calls out for him in the early morning hours, embraces his naked body,
        tight like coral, soft as marsh grass, recognizes they are the
in-betweeners growing toward the sea surface, like a ring of pink coral,

neither on land nor sea, they live in a space between. On their atoll bed
        they love once again, their eyes open, searching.

Cascade #32 Astronomer alone

A minor B cadence rang in his ears, woke him in the morning light
        after she left, after his night of stars and morning
coffee alone in a garden of a sloping jade succulent bern, after his

acceptance of the seven levels of matter, not denial, not anger,
        not bargaining, not depression a cadence then an oboe playing
Marcello Albononi as he waited for the night sky to open for Mira the

Variable Star, Capella, Urse Major to greet his eye alive into light. Doors
        to office, to house, unlocked, open windows in case
she returned, the phone by his side in case they're found, an oboe recording,

the night sky, hope, then silence. After her phone call, her words of departure,
        "I'll always love you," a coyote, his brown brush tail
cocked still, appeared in their lemon orchard watched him as he turned inside.

Cascade #33 Jibe Ho

Once as a young bride in late winter afternoon she's
        struck by hormones longing blow, a yearning
ache to have a baby, then the preparing, then their mother.

When that longing released in their birth, when death released
        her to longing again she imagined her unburied
dead wandering as Virgil spirits through gurgling currents,

in landscape fueled runnels, for perhaps 1000 years. She carried
        her uneaten food back to kitchen sink, back again
into water, thinking of how her children once swam in mountain

streams, ate her lamb cutlets and gulped down chocolate
        mousse in Limoges ramekins, as no tears came
as no tears fell. She imagined a hull below waterline, a bow

pulpit submerged, a keel upturned stuck on a reef and rock
        below where no sunlight except for flickering
blue and green and perhaps, a sock, a tee-shirt, a loosened belt.

Cascade #34 Cranes

She glides into water, swims out alone looks up to see
        sixteen cranes cross sand and dune.
Do they carry her dead son's souls? A rolling mist

lifts as cranes sweep into air fluttering wings of good
        and longevity, as if, in China
where they carry departed souls. She side-strokes into

ocean swells, lets her legs bite through the water. Right,
        then left arm lifts up and down then she turns
her head to the side to breathe in air. With each kick she

kicks away her fear. With each breath she kicks away her
        grief. Then she lets go like the flying crane.

Cascade #35 Day of the Memorial

Because the morning's dawn crossed over the night's sky
        to forget them, to forget the church
packed with shy frightened faces, remembering together

her boys. Because the Angel of Death forgot her took them
        instead, passed her by. Because she entered their
room raised her arms high over empty beds lifted them up

to give a blessing over pillows and bears -- her arms high as if
        reaching for a gymnast's iron bar. Because like
a whirligig fanning empty air she hummed the *Kyrie Eleison*,

then the *Sanctus*, then her body weaved, fell, crumpled,
        her hands over her face, into their beds,
into their boyish scent -- because she was their Mother.

Cascade #36 Flight

Inside she takes her purse, her cosmetics, no pictures,
        no goodbyes, moves at warp speed as the
stranger's Porsche idles outside and as he sleeps unaware

of her betrayal. Even at dawn when his toes mingled
        like a rope between her own, no celestial
stardust saved them. She flees into a stranger's arms

to cross the sea, like Helen, to leave him with the sea's
        mystery, with the night's stellar landscape,
without a fleet to follow her, to find her, to bring her back.

Cascade #37 Pasture

Star fuel runs out, a marriage runs out, gravity takes over and death
        appears full cold. His constant in the hour before Venus
arrived was the never moving North Star. The hour he awoke to see

her purse, her cosmetics, her coat, gone, rain, then the thunderstorms
        the lightening flash red sprite in the sky startled him,
the sky like him shrugging its shoulder as together a decision addressing

the dualities of change. While the sky trumpeted its chords of discord and joy
        her white faced, black shanked Appaloosa its leopard spotted
coat water drenched, fed in their pasture, churned the meadow fodder, balanced,

earth and sky. Finally, he called the Appaloosa mare in to take shelter.

Cascade #38 Day Person

Once he studied the stars, never awake to study
        the flight of birds, to act in attention,
so as to divine. Once he a juggler of space, stars,

lost promise changed his face, slowered his gait,
        slurred his speech. Each new day
the telescope stood in his yellow study slighted.

Each afternoon he rode the Appaloosa through
        lemon orchards, cantered up hillsides,
saddle sore until he returned home to stable then

to sleep. Day and Night's duality reversed like
        a cat and a dove in the shadows,
a lion and a bull in the ring, the fiery and the watery.

He changed from night person into day person. Across
        the waves of the sea, towards the hillsides,
the orchards, the meadow horse grazing, formed a circle,

an orb, an anima whole. His boys taken by the triumphal
        force of the sea left him the patience
of a solitary quest surrounded by sea, pastures and orchards

to believe in the evidence of his senses as he once believed
        in the telescope's secrets in the sky.

Cascade #39 Chopin's Prelude B Minor

The best meat is slaughtered at the waxing of the moon.
    The night his children did not come
home the moon like a cadence of wind, breath, spirit

drowned broken by a windmill sail boat. On their rooftop,
    blue tiles overlapped one on top of another
a pigeon, the Etruscan Bird of the Soul, cooed out for

the unseen, alone unable to resist, he wept. His night sky,
    his living dazzling cosmos, its grasping
puzzles, he understood in a moment, then he lost it all like the

mouth of dawn, swallowed into the sea, pools of death, pools
    within pools, his experience to ask questions
ceased. Left alone in a house where gauzy pearl white silk

chiffon drapes opened for a view of their inlet blue heron fed,
    her Appaloosa roamed, iris bloomed, he clouded
staggered in the early morning light to leave house and memory

to sit on her mare, no spur on his boot, no plan for the day, no feral glee,
    aimless to ride, sweet as Chopin's Prelude B Minor.

Cascade #40 Sentimental

Sentimental tunes on the radio, tear-welled father, trite excuse,
        who predicts the unseen? Who predicts the divorce?
Predictable, they divorce. Real as the dawn in the car's rear view

mirror, his face tucked under a pillow he weeps. Then spoons
        rocky road ice cream watches it swim in bourbon.
She packs her gun inside a bosom holster lets her heart weep

on her sleeve. Others coo over infant toes and blond puppy ears.
        Yellow roses left at the door. Ribboned Mother's Day
cards tossed. Her babes once sucked in repose, religion and logic

                rest while her buttercups, his stars and physics
cast aside like a cry
        within a cry an absent hymn to marriage hope.

Cascade #41 Competition

Touching the wither, where the last blond hairs of her mane
        rose, one twin took the curry comb to raze
the dirt, make circular motions to caress the mare's peach-soft

hair letting the brush sashay while his brother brushed
        the horse straight from head to hoof.
Together they lifted her hoof to cleanse the frog inside,

her smooth cushion, the place of pumping blood.
        The identical twins coaxed,
tickled the mare then fought who was to hold her

reins, who was to sit in front, who was to sit on the rump.
        Then swinging their legs over the horse,
sat together astride galloping across their pasture towards

the lazy sea. Later, one threw the tennis ball up just as
        his racket reached the small of his back,
another twin returned the serve to the far side of the court,

then lobbed another shot, then both tried never to let the other
        have a shot, win the game. Before in their
stroller side-by-side one held the other's hand like in the crib

together on their backs reaching out to take the other's fingers
        to grab it tight. At the end of the day on their
Mother's lap one nestled on her right hip the other nestled on her

        left hip, competition ceasing, cuddling beginning.

Cascade #42 Gambler

Their Granddaddy jokester, teller of tall tales,
        teaser, prankster, charmer with
his white as cement toothy smile, stone-wise

glint in his eye, his Irish carny laugh he
        persuaded, then took. Fled
four wives like a shark circling a sea lion

squirming, around swirling eels unstoppable like
        a wave-cascade. An opportunist,
he listened for the frog's choirs to cease, watched stock

graphs rise like tumbleweeds somersaulting across
        a desert then landed the deal,
leveraged the stock, bought the company, risked other's

fortunes to gain a fortune then held their mortgages,
        car registrations, paid their tuitions, her
painting lessons, his telescope, finally gambled with the

waves, the wind, the stars, took their children, to lose it all.

Cascade #43 Gallery Opening

She watched the stranger mount her painting of lilac
        wisteria gone wild in a white arbor
colonnade, cascading blossoms falling into a green,

blue-grey pond. Alongside her landscape, mounted
        in a Baroque gold gilt frame hung
the stranger's painting of two horses in full gallop,

a lonely ivory-fanged elephant charging. Finishing,
        the stranger offered her a bottle of water
then asked, "Can you imagine your life in the savannah

beside a waterfall eating strawberries looking upward
        to the slight lines to the points at moonrise
at midsummer then to midwinter's moonrise, with me?"

She pivoted towards him then to where loose ends
        meet, a place where persimmons
fall from a tree, finally, she answered, "Yes, I can."

Cascade #44 Kite Flying

"Mine is higher," one brother shouts to his twin
        while wind deflects like a sneeze
on the surface of his kite wing. He controls the

halyard pulls the kite to the left lets it swoop close
        enough crashing into his brother's
prism diamond, he shortens the line avoids his kite

then a terraced cliff, begins to reel it in, then runs, his
        feet skipping through sand, sea pebbles,
shallow pools to avoid the purple and crimson anemones

squeeze and suck then the cinnamon seaweed cascades then
        the white foaming dribble like a pebble
skimming on water. Together with their kites they leap, jump

become Baryshnikovs of the air, Albrechts in a celestial
        ballet, their kites climbing up with their gifts
of air, speed, divine red and white streamers somersaulting.

Running on the dust white beach the brothers shout and scream,
        "Stay away from mine." "Pull to the right."
"Watch out." Finally, they steer, then they deflect their planes

downward tethering them with cast-off driftwood to ground.

Cascade #45 The Visit

Inside the stranger's studio the grieving mother
        startled by his canvas with its
blond woman's head split in two between ear

and eye, a cubist's vision, like the sand boring
        down into an open wound. While
in another painting a blue crane in steel-blue torpor

preens waiting for a breeze to lift his wing to the sky
        to create a metaphor that answer her whys
and waiting like her for the next Ark to migrate from

this galaxy to another before the sun dies. She touches
        the paint on his canvases, he sees the
reflecting light in her eye, then she turns to him to paint

the story of her twins blending, the smeared eclipses,
        the shadows of life inside the green
and her holy past like a grasshopper on Saint Augustine

grass dimming in pale green shadows. In wonder the stranger
        moves his arm to flirt with her breast, his smile
mingles with his smell then the water in his mouth, then the

swoosh of air, then again, finally his kiss reviving like sunlight.

Cascade #46 Flamenco

Be sure to gather your fingers together:
        pinky first,
pull in the second, third, a fourth finger
        tightly into your palm.

Twist wrist inward,
                outward,
                gather and release fingers,
                as you move your arm up like a steel sword firm across hip,
waist, up   to chest undulating each hand,
twisting wrists gathering fingers upward until
                a halo forms over your ears.

When castanets are between your fingers,
your masculine left,
                your feminine right,
one for harmony,
the other for melody,

      click   click
                then swing them

together to hear their ricochet release.

Heels to floor,

      stomp, stomp, stomp,

your miguelitos steel tap toes ring
like gunshots onto the wooden floor.

A flamenco crescendo:
your hips shimmy,
hands twist,
fingers gather,
head turns left,
your petticoat's red and white flounces sway.

Smelling Sevilla.
                Hearing Conte Jondo.

Remembering Lorca.

                            Feeling duende.

Forgetting your age.

Cascade #47 Know Your Knots

      Start with a lark's head knot.
Bring far left cord over two middle cords and under far right one,
      like how coffee is made for you, breakfast eggs, buttered toast.

Pull tight. Don't let cords twist,
      like the days after the memorial,
      the cleaning out of closets,
      letters of sympathy to answer.

Follow with a square knot tied over and over in a tight repeat.
Learn this knot to remember when you wash,
slip and sooth in Epsom salted bath to loosen then weep,
      then repeat.

          Alternate square knots
        and make a diamond pattern
      to start with eight cords,
      tie rows of square knots,
      alternate cords with each to cover you,
      to cover up,
      to cover him.

Wind simple knots into a twist.
      Make a pattern.
      A knot cover for
      you to twist each year into the next
      knot,
      to follow to the next pattern.

        Repeat.

Then repeat again. Know your knots.

ABOUT THE AUTHOR

Joan Canby has an MFA from Vermont College of Fine Arts. Her poetry has been published in *Poetry South, Forage, Place Journal, California Quarterly, The Hawaiian Advertiser, Illyas Honey, Texas Observer, Forces, Beginnings, New Voices, Cape Rock, Voices Project, Brevitas, Broken Plate, Main Street Rag, Presence* and *Thema*. Her chapbook *Metaxe* was published in 2010 about the Holy Land. Her stories and articles have appeared in numerous magazines, including *International Society for Performance Instruction, Society of Technical Communicators, Mature Living, Women's Circle, Yankee Horseman's Pedlar, Road Rider, Modus Operandi,* and *Noticias Santa Barbara Historical Society*. She was the recipient of a second-place prize in biography from the National Society of Arts and Letters (NSAL) for her biography of Marie Louise, Empress of France and Archduchess of Parma. Her chapbook, *Write of Divorce*, was a quarterfinalist for the Mary Ballard Chapbook 2013 contest. Her chapbook of 27 Pantoums, *Sunrise to Moonlight*, was a semifinalist for the Mary Ballard Chapbook 2014 contest. She lives in Dallas, TX.

www.ingramcontent.com/pod-product-compliance
Lightning Source LLC
Chambersburg PA
CBHW021431070526
44577CB00001B/167